32
Seafood
Dishes

By Marie Bianco

BARRON'S

Woodbury, New York • Toronto • London • Sydney

© Copyright 1983 by Barron's Educational Series, Inc.

All inquiries should be addressed to:

Barron's Educational Series, Inc.
113 Crossways Park Drive
Woodbury, New York 11797

International Standard Book
No. 0-8120-5530-6

Library of Congress Catalog Card
No. 83-2690

Library of Congress Cataloging in Publication Data
Bianco, Marie.
  32 seafood dishes.

  (Barron's easy cooking series)
  Includes index.
  1. Cookery (Seafood) I. Title. II. Title:
Thirty-two seafood dishes. II. Series.
TX747.B44 1983   641.6'9   83-2690
ISBN 0-8120-5530-6

PRINTED IN THE
UNITED STATES OF AMERICA
3 4 5   RAE   9 8 7 6 5 4 3 2 1

Credits

Photography
Color photographs: Irwin Horowitz
Food preparation: Andrea Swenson
Stylist: Hal Walter

Food writer Marie Bianco is a food writer for Long Island's *Newsday*.
Cover and book design   Milton Glaser, Inc.
Series editor   Carole Berglie

INTRODUCTION

It used to be said that fish was brain food, and although we now know that there isn't any direct relationship, it still makes good sense to eat fish. Seafood in general is low in calories, low in cholesterol, and high in unsaturated and polyunsaturated fatty acids. That's good news to weight-conscious Americans and to those concerned with the health problems associated with the high incidence of heart disease in this country. Studies have proved that eating fish can have excellent results in helping reduce the amount of triglycerides and saturated fats in diets.

In addition to being low in the things people wish to avoid, fish is high in those nutrients we very much need: protein, essential amino acids, and minerals. For the peoples of the world, fish constitutes the second most important category of food, the first being cereals (not meat, as you might have thought!). The average American consumes about 11 pounds of fish annually, but that number is increasing as more people discover seafood.

What is good for you often is dull and tasteless, but with fish you get high nutrition *plus* delicious eating. We think you'll find each of these recipes an inviting sample of the sea's bounty, a treat for everyone's taste. And all fish and shellfish do not taste alike, nor are all seafood preparations tediously complex. Here you'll find simple but exciting uses for common fish and shellfish, such as the delicate Crab-stuffed Fillets on Spinach Noodles (p. 17) or the spicy Escabeche of Fish (p. 55), a marinated mixture of fish, peppers, chilies, and herbs. The French classic—Bourride—is brought to you without fuss: it's a robust, creamy white fish stew served with a garlicy mayonnaise (p. 31). The Scallop Chowder (p. 62) offers an intriguing diversion from the usual clam concoction.

For an appetizer, consider the Baked Clams, with their crusty tops enclosing a filling chock full of succulent clam meat (p. 19). Or have the Dutch Herring Salad (p. 62), a simple preparation that can be mixed up in only minutes, then kept chilled until your guests arrive. The Striped Fish Pâté (p. 47) is for special occasions, with its layers of delicate whitefish sandwiching strips of salmon fillet.

When you plan a simple family meal, consider the Mixed Seafood Casserole (p. 9), a hearty dish that comes bubbling from the oven ready to be enjoyed. Or the Salmon-vegetable Chowder (p. 39) for that Sunday-night supper when you want to keep things easy. The Barbecued Fish Kabobs (p. 41) are perfect for summertime outdoor eating; these smokey fish cubes will win over the most avid meat-eater.

For a taste of America, there's the New England Fish Pie (p. 45), a favorite since colonial days. Or travel gastronomically to the Chesapeake Bay for Katherine's Crab Meat Cakes (p. 57). The Shrimp Jambalaya (p. 63) and the Fish Fillets with Creole Sauce (p. 21) will remind you of Louisiana, while the Cioppino (p. 15)—a hearty fish stew rich with tomatoes and herbs—takes your heart to San Francisco.

But fish is not solely an American favorite, so we've brought you some samples from other countries as well. For an Italian focus, try the Linguine with Red/White/Green Clam Sauce (p. 63). The Paella (p. 61) is Spanish in inspiration, while the Steamed Fish (p. 59) is a ginger-spiked oriental treat.

Whether you are tempted by the lobster-filled Crêpes (p. 35) or the salted Codfish Balls (p. 11), you'll find the preparations given simply, the ingredients readily available, and the flavors true and natural. Bait your appetite and cast your thoughts toward the sea—shall it be halibut tonight?   C.B.

SOME FISH TALES

When shopping for fresh fish, you will often find the highest quality as well as greatest value if you choose those kinds that are local and in season.

BUYING FISH

When buying fresh *whole fish,* look for bright, clear, and bulging eyes, gills showing red underneath, and firm and elastic flesh holding taut to an iridescent skin; the fish should not have a fishy odor.

Fish steaks are slices cut through the thickest part of large fish such as halibut, cod, or swordfish. The slices should be about 1 1/2 inches thick, with translucent and moist flesh. *Fish fillets* are harder to judge for freshness, but look for pieces that are firm, shiny, and moist; avoid any that are flaking apart.

BUYING SHELLFISH

When purchasing fresh shellfish, look for clams, oysters, and mussels that have tightly closed shells. Hard-shelled clams are in season all year, but steamers are best in the summer. Oysters are at their peak in all seasons except summer; mussels are available throughout the year.

Oysters and clams are also sold shucked and in containers along with some of their liquid. These are somewhat perishable, so use them within a few days. The color of oysters and their liquid will vary with diet; a pink color is no indication of age.

Scallops are sold usually out of the shell; they should be pearly and moist, never white and dry. Bay scallops from Long Island and Cape Cod are in season from September to April; other bay types are year-round, as are the larger sea scallops.

Most crabs and lobsters are bought live, so pick active ones (soft-shelled crabs are not as active as blue crabs); both lobsters and crabs are in season all year. Highly perishable lump crab meat is often sold fresh refrigerated; when also pasteurized, it keeps longer. If lobsters have been precooked, select ones with tightly curled tails, indicating they were alive when cooked. When choosing cooked crabs, watch for freezer burn—the shells will be dull white.

Raw shrimp are sold either fresh or thawed (frozen when caught). Your merchant should label them as such, but this is not always the case. Some people have a preference for the fresh, and often these are the ones with the heads left on; they are available mostly in the summer and fall. Whether fresh or thawed, the color of the shrimp is an indication only of its diet and cannot show freshness. Iodine taste traces the source and season of harvest, not its freshness.

FROZEN FISH

If fresh finfish and shellfish are not available to you, then you can still enjoy these recipes, if under more limited circumstances. There are great many varieties of fish now frozen and shipped throughout the country, and often these are of excellent quality. Keep frozen fish in your freezer until you intend to use it, then thaw it slowly in the refrigerator until flexible and easy to separate. If you must thaw it more quickly, wrap it in an airtight package and place it under cold running water. Never thaw fish in warm water or at room temperature, and never refreeze thawed fish.

COMMON VARIETIES OF FISH

BASS   There are both fresh- and saltwater fishes with this name. The freshwater ones include small- and large-mouthed and rock and black bass; they average 3 pounds, are meaty fish often broiled or baked. For saltwater bass, see Striped Bass and Sea Bass.

BLACKFISH   An inexpensive saltwater fish with silver-gray flesh; good broiled, baked, or sautéed.

BLUEFISH   An oily fish in season most of the year along the East Coast. Best baked whole or broiled as fillets.

CARP   A winter and spring freshwater favorite in many countries, this may sometimes have a muddy taste. With a meaty flavor, good baked or served with a sweet-sour sauce.

CATFISH   An all-season freshwater fish with a delicate flesh, especially good dusted with cornmeal and deep-fried.

COD   A large saltwater fish coming from colder waters, this has a plain taste and is used extensively commercially. Available all year as steaks and large fillets. Also salted for long-term storage. A baby cod is a Scrod.

FLOUNDER   Like sole, flounder is a light whitefish, usually sold in fillets. The taste is delicate and mild, the fillets small.

HADDOCK   Like cod, this is smaller but with a similar taste. Usually sold as fillets, and sometimes smoked (finnan haddie).

HALIBUT   A large saltwater fish, usually sold throughout the year as steaks; has a white flesh and sturdy flavor. The tasty baby halibuts are sometimes sold too, as are the cheeks (only on the West Coast).

MACKEREL   An oily fish, at its peak in spring and summer. Best grilled or baked; often marinated or smoked.

MONKFISH   Also called Anglerfish, this has a chunky, meaty texture that's good for braising and grilling.

OCEAN PERCH   Not an actual fish, but a term to refer to several types usually frozen for supermarket sales. Very bland, but with sturdy texture; almost boneless.

PIKE   Abundant in northern fresh waters, a fine-textured fish with a good flavor. Delicious broiled as steaks or baked as fillets. Also can be stuffed and baked or braised.

POLLACK   Similar to haddock or cod, often packaged and sold as "deep-sea fillets." Good a variety of ways.

RED SNAPPER   An impressive fish to serve whole because of its bright color; also sold year-round as large fillets. Mild flavor, good texture.

SALMON   The king of fish, both a salt- and freshwater fish depending on period of life. Flesh is firm and well textured, pink varying to light gray; taste is mild but unforgettable. Also served cold or smoked or canned. Pacific salmon is at its best in summer; Atlantic, all times except summer.

SCROD   A baby cod; firm-fleshed fillets usually prepared as any other whitefish.

SEA BASS   Averaging from 1/2 pound to 5 pounds, these are often cut into steaks or sold as fillets, mostly in summer and fall. Often marinated, baked with herbs and wine.

SEA TROUT   Also called Weakfish, with light gray flesh and somewhat strong flavor. Sold almost year-round as fillets or sometimes small whole fish.

SMELTS   Sweet-fleshed, very small fish that are best fried.

SOLE   A delicate flavor and texture, fillets are lightly sautéed or broiled or baked; available throughout the year.

STRIPED BASS   Also known as Rockfish, good for stuffing and baking; best in summer and fall.

SWORDFISH   The classic fish steak, very firm and often dry; prepare it with a sauce. At its peak in summer and fall.

TILE FISH   With a mild shellfish flavor, a year-round favorite as fillets and small steaks.

TROUT   Small and beautiful, delicate flavor best sautéed whole or grilled.

TUNA   Dark and meaty steaks and fillets; the fish is oily but with a pleasant, haunting flavor; sold mostly in summer.

YIELD

6 servings

PREPARATION

20 minutes

COOKING

15 minutes

INGREDIENTS

6 tablespoons butter or margarine
¼ cup chopped onion
2 tablespoons chopped shallots
I clove garlic, minced
1½ pounds scallops
Salt and pepper
¾ cup all-purpose flour
I tablespoon olive oil
⅔ cup dry white wine
I small bay leaf
⅛ teaspoon thyme
¼ cup grated swiss cheese

In a small saucepan melt 2 tablespoons of butter and cook onion 5 minutes ①; do not brown. Add shallots and garlic and cook I minute longer. Set aside.

Wash scallops and pat dry ②. Cut into ¼-inch slices ③. Season with salt and pepper and dredge in flour, brushing off any excess.

In a skillet heat 2 tablespoons butter with the olive oil and sauté scallops lightly. Add wine, bay leaf, thyme, and cooked onion mixture. Cook for 5 minutes, then discard bay leaf.

Remove scallops with slotted spoon. Raise heat and boil rapidly to reduce liquid and thicken sauce. Return scallops to pan. Taste for seasoning.

Divide scallop mixture evenly among 6 buttered scallop shells. Sprinkle with cheese and dot with remaining butter. Place on a broiler-proof pan.

Run pan under broiler for 3 to 4 minutes to heat through and brown cheese lightly.

MIXED SEAFOOD CASSEROLE

YIELD
8 servings

PREPARATION
15 minutes

COOKING
25 minutes

INGREDIENTS

½ pound lump crab meat
6 ounces cooked lobster meat
½ pound shrimp, cooked, shelled, and
    deveined
4 tablespoons butter or margarine
½ pound sliced fresh mushrooms
2 cups hot cooked rice
1 cup sour cream
1 cup ricotta
2 tablespoons dry white wine

2 tablespoons finely chopped green
    pepper
2 tablespoons chopped scallions
1 tablespoon Worcestershire sauce
Salt
Dash of cayenne
¼ cup grated parmesan cheese
¼ cup bread crumbs

Preheat oven to 350 degrees. Pick over crab meat and remove any cartilage. Cut lobster into chunks. Cut shrimp in half.

Place seafood into a large bowl. Heat 2 tablespoons butter in a small skillet and sauté mushrooms 5 minutes ①. Add to seafood.

Gently fold in rice, sour cream, ricotta, wine, green pepper, scallions, Worcestershire sauce, salt, cayenne, and parmesan cheese ②. Spoon mixture into a buttered 2-quart casserole. Heat remaining 2 tablespoons butter and mix with bread crumbs and sprinkle over top ③.

Bake until hot and bubbly, about 20 minutes.

CODFISH BALLS

YIELD
6 servings

PREPARATION
15 minutes

SOAKING
5–7 hours

COOKING
15 minutes

INGREDIENTS
1 pound salted fish
6 to 8 potatoes
½ teaspoon pepper
2 eggs
Vegetable oil for frying

Place cod in a bowl, cover with water ①, and soak for several hours, changing water a few times. Drain and cut into ¾-inch cubes. There should be about 2 cups.

Peel potatoes and cut into ¾-inch cubes. You should have about 4 cups.

Place potatoes in a large saucepan, cover with water, and cook until potatoes are tender. Drain thoroughly.

Mash potatoes and cod together with a potato masher. Add pepper and eggs and beat with an electric mixer until light and fluffy. Taste the mixture and add salt, if necessary.

Preheat oven to 300 degrees. Fill a deep skillet with oil to the depth of ½ inch. Slip a tablespoon of mixture into oil ② and cook until light brown, about 1 minute, turning once ③. Drain on paper towels. Keep warm in oven, uncovered, until all are made.

NOTE *For this recipe, you could use salted cod, haddock, halibut, or pollack—the type purchased in a wooden box in the refrigerator section of your market.*

YIELD
4 servings

PREPARATION
10 minutes

COOKING
45 minutes

INGREDIENTS
2 cups water
¾ cup dry white wine
3 whole peppercorns
½ cup thinly sliced carrots
¼ cup chopped scallions
1 tablespoon chopped Italian (flat)
   parsley
¾ teaspoon salt
½ teaspoon dried tarragon
1 clove garlic
1 cup sliced fresh mushrooms

1 cup heavy cream
1½ tablespoons cornstarch
4 fish steaks

In a large, deep skillet combine water, wine, peppercorns, carrots, scallions, parsley, salt, tarragon, garlic, and mushrooms. Bring to a boil, reduce heat and simmer, uncovered, for 30 minutes.

Discard the garlic and peppercorns. Blend cream and cornstarch; add to saucepan ①. Cook, stirring constantly, until mixture thickens.

Add fish steaks to skillet and spoon sauce over them ②. Simmer 15 minutes or until fish flakes when pierced with fork ③.

NOTE For this recipe, use salmon, halibut, or tile fish steaks, about ½ pound each.

YIELD
6 servings

PREPARATION
15 minutes

COOKING
1 hour, 5 minutes

INGREDIENTS

¼ cup olive oil
1 cup chopped onions
3 cloves garlic
1 can (28 ounces) crushed tomatoes
1 can (6 ounces) tomato paste
1 cup chopped green pepper
1 teaspoon dried oregano
1 teaspoon dried basil
2 cups dry red wine
Salt and freshly ground black pepper
2 pounds firm-fleshed fish

½ pound sea scallops
½ pound shrimp
1 dozen littleneck clams or mussels, scrubbed well
¼ pound lump crab meat

In a large heavy stockpot, heat oil and sauté onions and garlic for 5 minutes.

Add tomatoes, tomato paste, green pepper, oregano, basil, wine, salt, and pepper. Bring to a boil, cover, lower heat, and simmer for 30 minutes.

Cut the fish into 2-inch pieces ①. Cut the scallops in half ②. Shell and devein the shrimp ③.

Add the fish to the stockpot, cover, and cook for 15 minutes. Add the scallops, shrimp, clams or mussels, and crab meat. Cover and simmer for 15 minutes.

NOTE For this recipe, use cod, tile fish, red snapper, striped bass, or halibut.

6

YIELD
6 servings

PREPARATION
35 minutes

COOKING
40 minutes

INGREDIENTS

8 ounces crab meat, fresh or frozen
½ cup finely chopped celery
2 tablespoons butter or margarine
¼ cup chopped scallions
2 tablespoons chopped Italian (flat)
    parsley
1 tablespoon lemon juice
¼ teaspoon salt
⅛ teaspoon black pepper
¼ teaspoon dill weed
6 fillets
Salt and pepper
2 cups spinach noodles, cooked and
    drained

2 tablespoons grated parmesan cheese

SAUCE

3 tablespoons butter or margarine
2 tablespoons all-purpose flour
½ teaspoon salt
⅛ teaspoon pepper
1 cup half-and-half
1¼ cups milk
2 egg yolks, beaten
2 tablespoons dry sherry

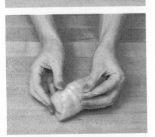

Pick over crab and remove any cartilage.

Sauté celery in butter; add crab and scallions, parsley, lemon juice, salt, pepper, and dill weed. Place a spoonful of crab stuffing on each fillet and spread into an even layer ①. Starting at the narrow end, roll up fillets ② and fasten with toothpicks ③.

To make the sauce, melt the butter and blend in flour, salt, and pepper. Add half-and-half and milk. Cook, stirring constantly until thickened and smooth. Add a small amount of the sauce to the egg yolks and return to sauce. Stir in sherry; cook over low heat 2 to 3 minutes.

Preheat oven to 350 degrees. Combine spinach noodles with 1½ cups sauce and grated parmesan cheese. Place in a buttered casserole and top with stuffed fish fillets. Cover and bake in oven for 30 minutes. Serve remaining sauce over fillets.

NOTE For the fillets, use sole, flounder, scrod, or any other firm-fleshed fish.

YIELD
6 servings

PREPARATION
25 minutes

COOKING
10 minutes

INGREDIENTS

18 cherrystone clams
1½ cups unseasoned bread crumbs
2 cloves garlic, finely minced
2 tablespoons finely chopped Italian
    (flat) parsley
Freshly ground pepper
Salt
½ teaspoon oregano
½ cup olive oil
4 tablespoons parmesan cheese

Wash clams and shuck them ①. Remove clam meat, drain, and chop fine ②. Wash 18 shell halves and set them aside. Preheat the oven to 450 degrees.

Divide the clam meat among the 18 shells. Place on a cookie sheet.

In a medium bowl combine bread crumbs, garlic, parsley, pepper, salt, and oregano. Add sufficient olive oil to hold mixture together. Divide mixture among shells, covering chopped clams completely ③. Sprinkle parmesan cheese over bread crumb mixture.

Bake clams in hot oven for 10 minutes. Run under broiler for a few seconds to brown. Serve as an appetizer, with lemon wedges if desired.

YIELD
4 servings

PREPARATION
15 minutes

MARINATING
2 hours

COOKING
50 minutes

INGREDIENTS
1 pound fish fillets
1/3 cup olive oil
1/3 cup dry white wine
2 tablespoons lemon juice
1 clove garlic, minced
1 teaspoon dried tarragon
1/2 teaspoon black pepper

CREOLE SAUCE
1/4 cup olive oil
1/3 cup chopped green pepper
1/3 cup chopped onion

1 clove garlic, chopped
3 large ripe tomatoes, peeled, seeded,
   and chopped
1/4 cup dry red wine
3 tablespoons tomato paste
1 tablespoon chopped green chili
1 teaspoon dried tarragon
1/2 teaspoon salt
1/4 teaspoon black pepper
1/4 cup sliced black olives
Hot cooked rice

Place fish in a shallow glass dish. Combine olive oil, wine, lemon juice, garlic, tarragon, and pepper; pour over fish ① and marinate for at least 2 hours in refrigerator. Drain, discarding marinade.

In a large, deep skillet heat olive oil and sauté green pepper, onion, and garlic ②. Add tomatoes, wine, tomato paste, green chili, tarragon, salt, and pepper. Bring to a boil and cook, stirring occasionally, 5 mintues ③. Lower heat, cover, and simmer 25 minutes.

Add fish fillets and olives to sauce. Cover and poach 15 minutes or until fish is opaque and flakes easily with fork. Serve with rice.

NOTE *For this recipe, use haddock, cod, tile fish, or bass fillets.*

YIELD
6 servings

PREPARATION
15 minutes

COOKING
20 minutes

CHILLING
5–7 hours

INGREDIENTS

2 cups water
3 chicken bouillon cubes
1 cup rice, uncooked
1 can (7 ounces) water-packed tuna
2 tablespoons vegetable oil
1/3 cup chopped scallions
2 teaspoons curry powder
3 tablespoons lemon juice
3 tablespoons vinegar
3 tablespoons olive oil
2 cloves garlic, finely minced

Lettuce leaves
1 avocado, peeled, seeded, and sliced
1 tomato, cut in wedges
Lemon slices and parsley for garnish
Condiments: chopped cucumber,
    sieved hard-cooked egg, chopped
    peanuts, crisp bacon bits

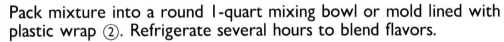

Place the water and chicken bouillon cubes in a medium saucepan. Bring to a boil and slowly add 1 cup rice. Cover and cook over low heat for 20 minutes. Cool slightly.

Drain and flake tuna. Combine with rice. Set aside.

In a skillet heat the vegetable oil and sauté scallions; remove and add curry powder to pan. Cook 1 minute, then blend in lemon juice, vinegar, olive oil, and garlic. Pour dressing over tuna-rice mixture. Mix in scallions and blend thoroughly ①.

Pack mixture into a round 1-quart mixing bowl or mold lined with plastic wrap ②. Refrigerate several hours to blend flavors.

Unmold onto lettuce-lined serving platter ③. Arrange avocado slices and tomato wedges around salad. Garnish with lemon slices and parsley. Serve with a selection of condiments such as cucumber, sieved egg, peanuts, and bacon bits.

23

YIELD
8 servings

PREPARATION
25 minutes

COOKING
1 hour

INGREDIENTS
1 dressed fish
Salt and pepper
2 tablespoons vegetable oil

STUFFING
4 tablespoons butter or margarine
½ cup chopped onion
½ cup chopped celery
½ teaspoon tarragon
½ teaspoon thyme
1 tablespoon chopped Italian (flat)
   parsley
2 cups fresh bread crumbs
Salt and pepper
12 oysters, shucked and in their liquid

Wash fish and pat dry. Sprinkle with salt and pepper. Wipe the outside of the fish with the vegetable oil ①. Place in a lightly greased baking pan. Preheat oven to 350 degrees.

In a large skillet melt butter. Add onion, celery, tarragon, thyme, and parsley and sauté 5 minutes.

Place onion mixture in a mixing bowl. Add bread crumbs, salt, and pepper to taste.

Drain oysters and place their liquid in a small saucepan. Heat to boiling. Cut oysters in half and place in hot liquid. Cook for 1 minute, then drain.

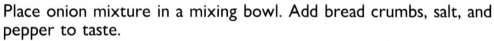

Add oysters to stuffing, along with 1 to 2 tablespoons of liquid to hold stuffing together ②.

Fill cavity of fish with stuffing ③. Secure with toothpicks. Bake in oven 50 to 60 minutes or until fish flakes easily.

NOTE For this recipe, use a 4- to 5-pound red snapper, bluefish, striped bass, sea trout, or small cod. The fish should be gutted and scaled, but the head left on.

YIELD
4 servings

PREPARATION
15 minutes

COOKING
25 minutes

INGREDIENTS

⅔ cup sliced almonds
4 tablespoons peanut oil
2 teaspoons chopped fresh ginger
1 pound firm whitefish fillets
3 tablespoons soy sauce
2 tablespoons cornstarch
1 large green pepper, seeded and cut
   into strips

1½ cups thinly sliced carrots
1½ cups zucchini, cut in ¼-inch slices
½ cup chicken broth
6 scallions with tops, cut in 1-inch
   lengths
3 cups hot cooked brown rice

In a large wok or skillet toss almonds and 1 tablespoon peanut oil until almonds are lightly browned, about 4 to 5 minutes ①. Stir in ½ teaspoon chopped ginger. Remove with slotted spoon to paper toweling to cool.

Halve the fish fillets; pat dry on paper toweling. Combine 1 tablespoon soy sauce with 1 tablespoon cornstarch. Brush on all surfaces of fish ②.

Heat 2 tablespoons of the remaining oil in wok and over medium high heat quickly sauté the fish on both sides until just cooked ③. Transfer to serving dish and keep hot.

Heat remaining 1 tablespoon oil in wok. Add pepper, carrots, and zucchini. Stir-fry over high heat for 2 to 3 minutes. Add chicken broth; cover and steam for 3 minutes.

Combine ¼ cup water with the remaining 2 tablespoons soy sauce, 1 tablespoon cornstarch, and 1½ teaspoons ginger. Reduce heat under wok to low and add soy mixture and scallions. Toss gently until sauce is slightly thickened, about 2 minutes. Spoon over fish. Sprinkle with almonds and serve with hot brown rice.

NOTE *For this recipe, use cod, halibut, or haddock fillets.*

27

YIELD
6 servings

PREPARATION
40 minutes

COOKING
25 minutes

INGREDIENTS

2 pounds fish fillets
1 package (10 ounces) frozen
   spinach, defrosted and drained
1/2 cup heavy cream
Salt and pepper
Dash of nutmeg
1/2 cup chicken broth

1/2 cup clam juice or white wine
6 ounces cooked shrimp
6 tablespoons butter
2 tablespoons all-purpose flour
2 tablespoons lemon juice

Preheat oven to 400 degrees. Wash fillets and pat dry. Combine spinach, 1 tablespoon heavy cream, salt, pepper, and nutmeg.

Lay fillets on a flat surface. Divide spinach mixture equally among them, spreading the mixture down the center of each fillet ①. Roll fillets up, pressing edges together so that the spinach cannot seep through ②.

Place fillets, seam side down, in a buttered baking pan. Pour in chicken broth and clam juice or white wine ③. Cover with a sheet of lightly buttered wax paper and poach in hot oven for 10 minutes.

Remove pan from oven and carefully poor off poaching liquid. If necessary, add more chicken broth or clam juice to make 1 cup. Set aside. (Fish can be prepared up to this point and refrigerated.)

Purée all but 3 shrimp in food processor by quickly switching it on and off 3 or 4 times, or chop it with a knife. Melt 4 tablespoons butter. With machine on, slowly pour in melted butter. Do not overprocess. If using knife, transfer shrimp to bowl and stir vigorously with fork to incorporate them.

Set oven to 350 degrees. In a small saucepan, melt remaining 2 tablespoons butter. Blend in flour, salt, and pepper to taste. Cook 2 minutes, stirring constantly.

Slowly add reserved poaching liquid and remaining heavy cream. Cook until slightly thickened, stirring constantly. Stir in lemon juice and shrimp-butter mixture.

Pour sauce over fish rolls. Cut remaining shrimp in half lengthwise and use as garnish for fish rolls. Bake in oven for 10 minutes, then serve.

NOTE Use fillets from a small fish, such as flounder, sole, or blackfish.

BOURRIDE—A FRENCH FISH STEW

YIELD
6 servings

PREPARATION
1 hour

COOKING
90 minutes

INGREDIENTS
6 pounds codfish, skin and bones
    removed and reserved
1/4 cup butter or margarine
1/3 cup light olive oil
4 leeks, chopped (white part only)
2 onions, sliced
6 carrots, diced
1 1/2 cups dry white wine
3 cups cold water
2 bay leaves
1 teaspoon crumbled thyme
1 teaspoon saffron threads
Salt and pepper

STEW
1/4 cup olive oil
2 onions, chopped
6 tomatoes, peeled, seeded, and
    chopped
6 leeks, chopped
1 celery heart, chopped
1/2 cup chopped fresh parsley
6 potatoes, peeled and diced
1/4 cup butter
1/4 cup olive oil
1 loaf French or Italian bread, cut into
    1/2-inch slices

SAUCE
1 cup mayonnaise, preferably
    homemade
4 cloves garlic, mashed

Separate boneless pieces of fish and skin, bones, head and tail. Place butter and olive oil into a large kettle. Heat mixture and sauté leeks, onions, and carrots until lightly browned ①. Stir in white wine, water, bay leaves, thyme, and saffron. Add fish skin, bones, head, and tail. Cover and simmer for 30 minutes. Strain and reserve broth ②. Season with salt and pepper. Discard bones and vegetables.

In the same kettle, heat olive oil and sauté onions until lightly browned. Add tomatoes, leeks, celery heart, parsley, and potatoes. Stir over low heat for 5 minutes. Place boneless pieces of fish on top of vegetables. Cover and simmer for 30 minutes or until fish is cooked and vegetables are tender. Place pieces of fish on platter and keep warm.

Pour vegetables into blender and whirl until smooth. Pour purée into large tureen. Heat reserved fish broth and stir slowly into vegetable purée . Season to taste with salt and pepper. Heat butter and oil and sauté bread slices on both sides.

In a bowl mix mayonnaise and garlic. Place a slice of bread and a piece of fish into a large soup bowl. Top with hot soup and a spoonful of mayonnaise mixture.

YIELD
6 servings

PREPARATION
15 minutes

COOKING
15 minutes

INGREDIENTS
1 pound smelts or other small fish
1 can (2 ounces) anchovy fillets
½ cup all-purpose flour
¼ teaspoon salt
⅛ teaspoon pepper
3 tablespoons butter or margarine
3 tablespoons vegetable oil
Lemon slices and dill sprigs for garnish

SAUCE
2 tablespoons minced onion
1½ tablespoons all-purpose flour
½ teaspoon salt
1¼ cups half-and-half
1 egg yolk, beaten
1 tablespoon lemon juice
1 tablespoon chopped fresh dill

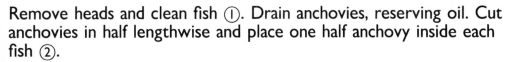

Remove heads and clean fish ①. Drain anchovies, reserving oil. Cut anchovies in half lengthwise and place one half anchovy inside each fish ②.

Combine flour with salt and pepper and roll each fish in it ③. Set aside.

To make sauce, heat reserved anchovy oil in a small saucepan. Add the minced onion and cook until tender, about 3 minutes. Blend in flour and salt. Gradually stir in half-and-half. Cook, stirring constantly, until thickened.

Add a little of the hot sauce to the egg yolk and return mixture to pot. Heat until thickened, stirring constantly. Add lemon juice and dill.

In a large skillet, melt butter and oil. Add fish, a few at a time, and cook until crisp, about 5 minutes.

Spoon sauce over fish, and serve on cooked rice. Garnish with lemon and dill.

YIELD

6 servings

PREPARATION

25 minutes

CHILLING

1 hour

COOKING

45 minutes

CRÊPES

1 cup all-purpose flour
1 ½ cups milk
2 eggs
1 tablespoon butter, melted
¼ teaspoon salt

FILLING

4 tablespoons butter or margarine
2 cups sliced fresh mushrooms
3 cups cooked lobster, cut into bite-
   size pieces

½ teaspoon salt
¼ teaspoon pepper
¼ teaspoon paprika
Dash of cayenne
2 cups half-and-half
½ cup dry sherry
3 egg yolks
2 tablespoons grated parmesan cheese
2 tablespoons grated swiss cheese

To make crêpes, place flour, milk, eggs, melted butter, and salt in a blender and process until smooth. Refrigerate for a minimum of 1 hour.

Heat a 7-inch frying pan and coat lightly with butter. Measure 2 tablespoons batter into pan ① and swirl it around quickly ②. Cook for 45 seconds and turn ③. Cook for 15 seconds on second side. Turn pan over and let crêpe drop onto wax paper. Repeat until all crêpes are made.

In a large skillet heat butter and sauté mushrooms; add lobster meat, salt, pepper, paprika, and cayenne. Mix well.

In a saucepan heat half-and-half to scalding, then add sherry. Beat egg yolks with a wire whisk. Beat a small amount of the half-and-half into the egg yolks and return to pan. Cook, over low heat, until slightly thickened. Do not boil.

Pour sauce over lobster/mushroom mixture and mix thoroughly.

Preheat oven to 350 degrees. Spread about ½ cup filling down center of each crêpe. Fold sides over and place, seam side down, in shallow pan. Pour any remaining sauce over crêpes. Combine parmesan and swiss cheese and sprinkle over crêpes. Place in oven for 20 minutes or until filling is hot and cheeses are melted.

YIELD
6 servings

PREPARATION
20 minutes

COOKING
1 hour

INGREDIENTS
1 dressed fish, about 4 pounds
1 teaspoon salt
2 tablespoons butter, melted

STUFFING
½ cup wild rice, uncooked
¼ cup butter or margarine
¼ cup chopped shallots
½ cup chopped celery
1 cup chopped fresh mushrooms
2 tablespoons chopped Italian (flat)
    parsley
Salt and pepper

Sprinkle fish inside and out with salt. Set aside.

To make stuffing, cook the wild rice in 4 cups water until tender, about 20 minutes. Drain and set aside. In a large skillet, melt the butter and sauté shallots and celery 3 minutes. Add mushrooms and cook 3 minutes longer. Add cooked wild rice, parsley, salt, and pepper to taste.

Preheat oven to 350 degrees. Fill fish cavity with stuffing ①. Close with toothpicks or skewers ②.

Brush fish with 1 tablespoon melted butter ③; place on a greased baking pan. Bake for 35 to 40 minutes or until fish flakes easily. Remove from oven and brush with remaining melted butter.

NOTE For this recipe use striped bass, bluefish, carp, or sea bass.

SALMON-VEGETABLE CHOWDER

YIELD
4 servings

PREPARATION
15 minutes

COOKING
35 minutes

INGREDIENTS

1 can (7¾ ounces) salmon
3 tablespoons bacon drippings or
    butter
½ cup chopped onion
½ cup chopped celery
¼ cup chopped green pepper
1 clove garlic, minced
1 cup diced potatoes
1 cup diced carrots
3 cups chicken broth
1 teaspoon salt

¾ teaspoon black pepper
½ teaspoon dill seed
½ cup diced zucchini
2 cups half-and-half
1 can (8¾ ounces) cream-style corn
Chopped parsley for garnish

Drain and flake the salmon, reserving liquid. Set both aside. In a large heavy pot, heat bacon drippings or butter and sauté onion, celery, green pepper, and garlic until transparent ①.

Add potatoes, carrots, chicken broth, salt, pepper, and dill seed. Cover, reduce heat to low, and simmer for 20 minutes. Add zucchini and cook 5 minutes.

Add flaked salmon, reserved salmon liquid, half-and-half, and corn. Heat thoroughly. Sprinkle with parsley.

NOTE To substitute fresh salmon, poach ½ pound piece of salmon in a cup of clam broth ② and use the clam broth instead of the salmon canning liquid. Drain and remove skin; flake meat from bones ③.

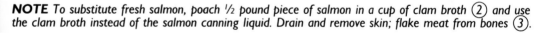

BARBECUED FISH KABOBS

YIELD
6 servings

PREPARATION
15 minutes

MARINATING
1 hour

GRILLING
10 minutes

INGREDIENTS
2 pounds thick firm fish, cubed
18 cherry tomatoes
18 small red potatoes, cooked
3 small zucchini, each cut into 6 chunks
18 large mushrooms
1 large onion, cut in half and separated
3 large green peppers, cut into 1-inch squares

MARINADE
½ cup vegetable oil
¼ cup soy sauce
1 teaspoon chopped fresh ginger
1 clove garlic, minced
Black pepper
2 tablespoons dry sherry

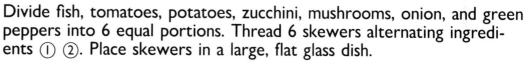

Divide fish, tomatoes, potatoes, zucchini, mushrooms, onion, and green peppers into 6 equal portions. Thread 6 skewers alternating ingredients ① ②. Place skewers in a large, flat glass dish.

Combine marinade ingredients and baste skewers ③. Marinate 1 hour, turning occasionally.

Barbecue over hot coals for 10 minutes or until fish is done. Turn skewers once and brush occasionally with marinade.

NOTE *These kabobs can also be broiled for the same amount of time. For the fish, use tuna, monkfish, pike, or sea trout.*

YIELD
4 servings

PREPARATION
25 minutes

COOKING
20 minutes

INGREDIENTS

12 large oysters
6 slices bacon
1/2 cup finely chopped onion
1/4 cup finely chopped celery
1/4 cup finely chopped green pepper
2 teaspoons lemon juice
1/2 teaspoon salt
1 teaspoon Worcestershire sauce
4 to 6 drops Tabasco

Shuck oysters ① ②, discarding any liquid. Wash and dry 12 oyster shells. Set aside. Preheat oven to 400 degrees.

In a medium skillet fry bacon until partially cooked. Add onion, celery, and green pepper and cook until tender. Add lemon juice, salt, Worcestershire sauce and Tabasco.

Arrange oysters in shells and place on a baking sheet. If the shells are not level, fill pan first with rock or kosher salt and settle the shells into the salt ③. Divide bacon mixture evenly over oysters. Bake in hot oven for 10 to 12 minutes or until edges of oysters begin to curl and topping is brown.

YIELD

4 servings

PREPARATION

20 minutes

COOKING

45 minutes

INGREDIENTS

1 pound fillets
1 cup water
1/4 teaspoon salt
1 bay leaf
4 tablespoons butter or margarine
2 tablespoons minced celery
2 tablespoons minced onion
4 tablespoons all-purpose flour
2 cups half-and-half
1/4 teaspoon dry mustard
1/4 cup chopped walnuts

1 tablespoon dry white wine
1 tablespoon pimiento
Pastry for 2-crust 9-inch pie

In a large skillet place fish fillets, water, salt, and bay leaf. Bring water to a boil, reduce heat, cover, and simmer for 6 to 8 minutes.

Carefully remove fish, drain, cool, and flake. Discard poaching liquid.

Heat butter and sauté celery and onion; stir in flour and cook over low heat for 30 seconds.

Add half-and-half and dry mustard and cook, stirring constantly, until mixture thickens. Remove from heat and stir in nuts, wine, pimiento, and flaked fish.

Preheat oven to 400 degrees. Spoon mixture into pastry-lined 9-inch pie pan ①. Cover with top crust ②, trim, seal edges, and flute. Trim with extra pastry, if desired. Cut steam vents in top crust ③. Bake in hot oven for 30 to 35 minutes or until top is browned. Allow pie to stand for 15 minutes before cutting.

NOTE For this recipe, use fillets of cod, pollack, haddock, or ocean perch.

STRIPED FISH PÂTÉ

YIELD
12 servings

PREPARATION
45 minutes

CHILLING
1 hour

BAKING
1 hour

RESTING
overnight

INGREDIENTS
2 pounds fish fillets
6 egg whites, lightly beaten
2 1/2 cups heavy cream
1 tablespoon chopped fresh parsley
1 tablespoon chopped fresh chives
2 teaspoons salt, or to taste
1 teaspoon chopped tarragon
1/2 teaspoon white pepper
dash of mace
dash of Worcestershire sauce
1/2 pound piece salmon fillet
2 tablespoons butter, melted

Pat fish fillets dry on paper toweling. Cut into cubes. Purée fish in food processor or grinder.

Transfer fish purée to mixing bowl. Slowly add egg whites to fish, beating well after each addition. Add cream a little at a time, beating until it is absorbed. Add parsley, chives, salt, tarragon, pepper, mace, and Worcestershire sauce. Refrigerate for 1 hour.

Preheat oven to 350 degrees. Cut salmon into thin strips.

Line a buttered 9 by 5-inch loaf pan with parchment ①. Butter parchment paper. Fill the pan with one third of the fish mixture and follow with half the salmon strips ②. Repeat; cover with the remaining fish mixture. Spread evenly and tap pan on counter to settle mixture. Brush top with melted butter and cover with aluminum foil.

Place pan in slightly larger pan filled with 1 inch of hot water ③. Bake in oven for 60 minutes. Remove loaf pan, cool slightly, and refrigerate overnight. Unmold, remove parchment paper, and serve.

NOTE *For this recipe, use cod, haddock, scrod, or striped bass.*

FISH STEAKS, LIVORNESE STYLE

YIELD
4 servings

PREPARATION
15 minutes

COOKING
35 minutes

INGREDIENTS

4 tablespoons olive oil
1½ pounds fish steaks
1 onion, chopped
2 cloves garlic, chopped
4 ripe tomatoes, peeled, seeded, and
    chopped
Salt and pepper
2 tablespoons chopped fresh Italian
    (flat) parsley

2 tablespoons capers, rinsed and
    drained
2 tablespoons chopped black olives

Preheat oven to 400 degrees. Use 1 tablespoon olive oil to grease a baking dish and a sheet of wax or parchment paper large enough to cover dish.

Place swordfish in dish, cover with more paper ①, and bake in oven for 10 minutes. Remove paper. Discard any excess liquid ②. Turn oven to 350 degrees.

In a large skillet, heat remaining olive oil and sauté onion and garlic until onion is transparent, about 4 to 5 minutes.

Add tomatoes, salt and pepper, parsley, capers, and olives to pan. Simmer for 15 minutes.

Spoon mixture over steaks ③, and bake 10 minutes or until fish flakes.

NOTE For the steaks, use tuna, swordfish, tile fish, cod, or bass.

YIELD
6 servings

PREPARATION
5 minutes

COOKING
15 minutes

INGREDIENTS
2 pounds fish fillets
1 cup dry white wine
2 tablespoons capers, rinsed and
    drained
1 tablespoon dijon-style mustard
½ cup heavy cream
1½ tablespoons cornstarch
2 tablespoons water

Preheat oven to 400 degrees. Wash fillets and pat dry. Arrange in buttered baking dish. Pour wine over fillets. Cut a piece of parchment paper to fit pan. Lightly butter the paper and cover fish with it.

Bake fish in hot oven for 10 minutes. Remove pan from oven. Carefully remove poaching liquid and pour into a small saucepan ①. (Fish can be prepared up to this point and refrigerated.)

Set oven to 350 degrees. Add capers and mustard to poaching liquid. Bring to a boil, lower heat, and simmer for 1 minute.

Stir heavy cream into mustard mixture. Combine cornstarch with water ② and slowly add to the sauce ③. Cook until slightly thickened.

Spoon sauce over fish and bake in oven for 10 minutes.

NOTE Use flounder, sole, striped bass, or bluefish fillets.

YIELD

6 servings

PREPARATION

15 minutes

COOKING

25 minutes

INGREDIENTS

2 tablespoons butter or margarine
3 scallions, minced
1 carrot, grated
1 clove garlic, minced
1 cup chopped fresh mushrooms
2 tablespoons chopped fresh Italian
  (flat) parsley
6 trout, about 8 ounces each
3 small zucchini, thinly sliced
Salt and pepper
1/2 teaspoon oregano

2 tablespoons lemon juice
2 tablespoons olive oil
1 lemon, thinly sliced

Preheat oven to 400 degrees. In a medium skillet melt butter and sauté scallions, carrot, and garlic for 3 minutes. Add mushrooms and parsley and cook another 2 minutes.

Wash trout and pat dry with paper toweling.

Divide sautéed vegetables into 6 equal portions and place 1 portion in cavity of each trout.

Place each trout on an oiled 12 by 15-inch piece of parchment paper or aluminum foil. Slide a few slices of zucchini under the trout and place a few on top.

Combine salt, pepper, oregano, and lemon juice and sprinkle it over the fish. Place a thin slice of lemon on each trout ①.

Bring up the 12-inch sides of the parchment and fold, drug store style ②. Fold edges of sides under with several folds ③. Place on a baking sheet and bake in hot oven for 15 to 20 minutes.

YIELD
12 servings

PREPARATION
15 minutes

COOKING
25 minutes

MARINATING
30 minutes

CHILLING
overnight

INGREDIENTS

2 pounds fish fillets
⅓ cup lime juice
2 cups all-purpose flour
2 tablespoons paprika
1 tablespoon salt
1 tablespoon pepper
¼ cup vegetable oil
2 onions, thinly sliced
2 medium green peppers, thinly sliced
2 small chilies, cut in fine strips
2 carrots, thinly sliced
2 bay leaves

2 cloves garlic, minced
1 teaspoon oregano
¼ teaspoon ground cumin
1 cup malt or cider vinegar
Olives and pimiento for garnish

Cut fish fillets into 1-inch cubes. Place in a shallow pan and cover with lime juice ①. Allow to stand 30 minutes, turning occasionally.

Combine flour, paprika, salt, and pepper. Drain fish cubes and dip into flour mixture, brushing off any excess.

Heat oil in a large skillet and sauté fish cubes over low heat until golden brown ②, about 15 minutes. Drain and arrange in a shallow dish.

Sauté onions in remaining oil in pan until limp, but not brown. Add green peppers, chilies, carrots, bay leaves, garlic, oregano, cumin, and vinegar. Heat to boiling point.

Pour vegetables and liquid in pan over fish ③. Cover and refrigerate 24 hours. Garnish with olives and pimiento.

NOTE Use sole, haddock, flounder, sea bass, sea trout, or scrod. This is best served as an appetizer.

YIELD
4 servings

PREPARATION
15 minutes

CHILLING
4–5 hours

COOKING
10 minutes

INGREDIENTS
1 pound crab meat
1 egg, lightly beaten
2 slices white bread, crumbled
½ teaspoon salt
½ teaspoon Old Bay seasoning
1 heaping tablespoon mayonnaise
   (approximately)
Vegetable oil

Pick through crab meat and remove any bits of shell or cartilage. Place one third of the crab meat in a bowl; add the egg and mix lightly with a fork. Add one crumbled slice of bread and toss lightly.

Add another one third of the crab meat to the bowl; toss lightly. Add the remaining crumbled bread and mix thoroughly but gently. Season with Old Bay seasoning. Mix in last third of the crab meat.

Stir in a heaping tablespoon mayonnaise ① and mix lightly. If the mixture is not holding together, add a small amount of mayonnaise. The mixture should just hold together. Shape into 8 crab cakes ②. Place on a dish and cover with plastic wrap. Chill for several hours.

Pour into an electric fry pan enough vegetable oil to cover bottom slightly. Heat to 350 degrees and fry crab cakes ③ until crusty on both sides.

YIELD
4 servings

PREPARATION
20 minutes

COOKING
40 minutes

INGREDIENTS

I 3-pound fish, dressed
3 tablespoons peanut oil
I teaspoon minced fresh ginger
Salt and pepper
3 cloves garlic, minced
½ cup scallions (white part and
   I inch of green)
I green pepper, seeded and cut into
   I-inch squares
½ cup packed brown sugar
½ cup red wine vinegar

3 tablespoons soy sauce
2 ripe tomatoes, quartered
I tablespoon cornstarch
2 tablespoons water
Hot cooked rice

Slash fish every 2 inches on both sides, about ¼ inch deep ①. Combine peanut oil and ginger and rub it into fish ②. Sprinkle with salt and pepper.

Place fish on a 16-inch baking rack in a large pot with cover. Add ½ inch water to pot ③ and bring to a boil. Lower heat, cover, and simmer for 25 minutes or until fish is tender. Do not turn during time of steaming. Remove fish to a platter and keep warm.

To make sauce heat remaining tablespoon peanut oil in medium skillet. Stir-fry garlic, scallions, and pepper for 5 minutes. Stir in brown sugar, vinegar, and soy sauce and cook until sugar is dissolved.

Add tomatoes to skillet. Stir cornstarch and water together, then add to skillet and cook until mixture is slightly thickened. Pour on fish and serve over rice.

NOTE Use pike, bass, or flounder.

SHRIMP, CLAM, AND MUSSEL PAELLA

YIELD
6 servings

PREPARATION
10 minutes

COOKING
40 minutes

INGREDIENTS

¼ cup olive oil
1 large onion, chopped
2 cloves garlic, chopped
1½ cups rice, uncooked
⅛ teaspoon saffron
1 bottle (8 ounces) clam juice
3 cups chicken broth, canned or
   homemade (approximately)
1 bay leaf
1 pound shrimp, shelled and deveined
18 littleneck clams, scrubbed well

18 mussels, scrubbed well
1 cup peas, fresh or frozen
2 tablespoons chopped pimiento
Salt and pepper

In a large skillet, heat oil and sauté onion and garlic until soft. Add rice and saffron and cook 5 minutes, stirring constantly ①. Add clam juice, 2 cups chicken broth, and bay leaf to skillet and simmer, covered, for 10 minutes.

Remove cover, stir in 1 additional cup chicken broth and shrimp. Cover and cook 5 minutes. Remove cover and add additional chicken broth if rice is dry.

Add clams and mussels to rice mixture and poke them into the rice ②. Cover and cook 10 minutes or until they open; discard any that do not open. Add peas and pimiento ③. Season with salt and pepper. Reheat and serve.

DUTCH HERRING SALAD

YIELD

8 servings

PREPARATION

5 minutes

COOKING

1 hour

INGREDIENTS

2 jars herring tidbits in wine sauce, diced and liquid reserved
2 cups unpeeled diced Delicious apples
1½ cups chopped onions
1½ cups sliced cooked potatoes
1½ cups diced cooked beets

2 tablespoons capers, rinsed
½ cup mayonnaise
½ cup sour cream

In a large bowl combine diced herring, apples, onions, potatoes, beets, capers, mayonnaise, sour cream and 2 tablespoons liquid from herring jar. Mix well and refrigerate for at least 1 hour.

SCALLOP CHOWDER

YIELD

4 servings

PREPARATION

10 minutes

COOKING

30 minutes

INGREDIENTS

1 pound scallops
4 ounces salt pork, diced
1 cup sliced onions
Butter (optional)
3 cups clam broth
2 cups diced potatoes
1 teaspoon salt

½ teaspoon freshly ground black pepper
2 cups light cream
Pilot crackers

Wash and dry scallops. If using sea scallops, cut in half; leave bay scallops whole.

In a large stockpot, sauté salt pork until crisp. Drain and set aside. Sauté scallops in pork fat for 3 minutes. Remove scallops and set aside. Sauté onions in same pan, adding a small amount of butter, if necessary.

In a medium saucepan, heat clam broth. Add potatoes, salt, and pepper. Simmer for 15 minutes or until potatoes are tender.

To onions in stockpot add cooked scallops, potatoes, clam broth, and salt pork bits. Heat to simmer; do not boil. Serve with pilot crackers.

LINGUINE WITH RED/WHITE/GREEN CLAM SAUCE

YIELD
4 servings

PREPARATION
10 minutes

COOKING
30 minutes

INGREDIENTS

1 pound linguine
2 cans (6½ ounces each) minced
   clams
¼ cup olive oil
1 onion, chopped
3 cloves garlic, minced
½ teaspoon dried oregano
½ teaspoon dried basil or
   2 tablespoons chopped fresh basil

2 tablespoons chopped Italian (flat)
   parsley
1 ripe tomato, peeled, seeded, and
   chopped
Grated parmesan cheese
Red pepper flakes

Cook linguine according to package directions. Drain.

Open clams and drain liquid; reserve.

In a medium saucepan, heat olive oil and sauté onion and garlic 5 minutes. Do not brown. Add clam liquid, oregano, basil, parsley, and tomato. Simmer 10 minutes.

Add clams and heat, but do not boil. Pour sauce over drained pasta. Serve with parmesan cheese and pepper flakes.

SHRIMP JAMBALAYA

YIELD
4 servings

PREPARATION
10 minutes

COOKING
45 minutes

INGREDIENTS

1 pound shrimp
4 slices bacon, cut in 1-inch pieces
1 onion, chopped
1 large green pepper, cut in 1-inch
   squares
2 cloves garlic, minced
1 cup rice, uncooked
2 cups canned crushed tomatoes

1 cup water
¼ teaspoon salt
1 bay leaf
½ teaspoon thyme
Cayenne pepper
1 cup diced boiled ham
¼ cup chopped Italian (flat) parsley

Shell the shrimp and devein, if desired.

In a large skillet, sauté bacon. Remove and drain. In bacon fat sauté onion, green pepper, and garlic for 3 minutes. Add rice and cook 5 minutes, stirring constantly.

Add crushed tomatoes, water, salt, bay leaf, thyme, and cayenne to taste. Cover and cook 15 minutes. Add shrimp and ham and combine well. Add ½ cup additional water, if necessary. Cover and cook 10 minutes or until rice is cooked. Remove bay leaf. Sprinkle with parsley and bacon, and serve.

INDEX